# THE MOVE

### How to Get Rid of All That Stuff and Downsize.

Sharon Canfield Dorsey

Blessings

Sharon

Thank you for choosing to purchase an authorized edition of *The Move - How To Get Rid Of All That Stuff and Downsize.*

High Tide's mission to find, encourage, promote, and publish authors' work. We are a small, woman-owned enterprise dedicated to authors over 50. When you buy an authorized copy, you not only support us but also gain access to a unique edition that is a testament to your commitment to our cause.

By respecting copyright law and refraining from reproducing or scanning any part of our work without our written permission, you not only protect our authors' rights but also play a crucial role in enabling us to continue supporting them, publishing their work, and delivering it to you for your enjoyment.

Printed in the United States.

Published by
High Tide Publications, Inc.
Deltaville, Virginia 23043
www.HighTide Publications.com

ISBN 978-1-962935-03-6

# Contents

# You're What?!?

What 80-year-old woman in her right mind would want to leave her 3,100 sq. ft. home of seventeen years to downsize into a town-home, especially when that beautiful home was filled with priceless memories, art collections, and was situated on two wooded acres?

Maybe a woman who was tired of constant repairs, of deer who ate her flowers, of squirrels who carried off her apples, and neighbor chickens who pooped on her sidewalk. Hmmm.

So, in May, 2023, I woke up one morning and decided it was time. Just like that! No conversations with children. No "should I?" or "shouldn't I?" just a certainty that this was the right time to make the change.

This is my story.

*$15,000 seemed an unreasonable amount of green for maintaining my woodsy abode. It could buy a lot of tickets to faraway places!*

# The Decision

My husband died ten years ago. Living in the home we shared kept him alive for me, gave me a feeling of continuity, security, and provided a beautiful place to store all the memories and mementos of twenty years of travel and adventure. I always told my friends and family that I loved my home and would live in it until carried out, feet first.

That decision to remain there was reinforced during the pandemic years. My friends who had already downsized and moved into retirement communities or assisted living facilities were held prisoner in their tiny apartments through the COVID years. On the other hand, I had lots of rooms to roam and two acres of wooded splendor to enjoy. I felt pretty superior as they whined and lamented their choices.

Then, I was hit squarely in the face with a dose of reality in the form of my 80th birthday. My daughter gifted me with a sparkly crown and a lovely sash that said, "Eighty is fabulous!" But was it? Serious back issues had made it impossible for me to care for the yard. My 40-year-old house, though lovely, required constant repairs and replacements – kind of like me. When I totaled up the financial damage at the end of the year for repairs and yard work, $15,000 seemed an unreasonable amount of green for maintaining my woodsy abode.

That $15,000 could buy a lot of tickets to faraway places or make a down payment on a grandkid's first year of college. Did I really need all that space and all those woods? What did they provide – deer that ate my flowers; rabbits that consumed everything the deer missed; squirrels that stripped the apple and pecan trees; a peacock who lived next door but flew over the fence to chase me every time I tried to cut flowers in the garden; chickens from my other next door neighbor who visited each day to peck holes in the Styrofoam faucet covers; and mice who somehow found their way inside, probably trying to escape the black snake, who followed them in and curled up on my white carpet at the bottom of the living room stairs.

I respect Mother Nature's pecking order, but, really? In my living room? Even then, I couldn't quite decide to give it all up.

The next shoe to drop was a horrific year of auto-immune difficulties for me, triggered, the puzzled doctors tentatively decided, by my third COVID shot. My symptoms ranged from body rashes, to blisters on my face, to outbreaks of psoriasis; to eye infections – the list went on, and the weird symptoms kept coming. I would get one thing cleared up, and another would surface. I felt depressed and defeated.

One day, my wise friend, Kaye, reminded me that physical symptoms can evolve from stress, which I knew and acknowledged, but also from fear. Fear? What did I have to fear? I have a great job as a Mary Kay Cosmetics Sales Director. I just celebrated 42 years of making women more beautiful and more prosperous. I am a poet/writer and have published twelve well-received books. I have two great kids w/lovely spouses, three amazing grandchildren and more friends scattered across the country than I can keep up with. Life is good! I even have t-shirts that proclaim same. I went to sleep that night, asking myself that

question – what am I afraid of? What is making me anxious?

I woke up the next morning with the answer. It's the house! It was no longer a haven of beauty and tranquility. It was a blood-sucking demon, demanding my constant attention and consuming my money like a voracious caterpillar. It was time to cut it loose!

4

# THE PLAN

Day 2 of the move was a reality check. Never one to wallow in uncertainty, I jumped right in and called my neighbor, Chelle, who's a realtor. She was shocked and a little sad that I was leaving the community. We had been on the HOA board of directors together and developed a lot of respect for each other. That's why I chose her. I knew I could trust her to guide me through this daunting ride. Plus, she was smart, fun, and a genuinely good person.

Her first question was, "Where do you want to go?"

It was an easy answer. "My first choice would be a townhouse in my daughter, Shannon's community, Williamsburg Village at Norge. It's a pretty neighborhood – small, quiet and has trees. I will still have my greenery but someone else would take care of it. "I need three bedrooms, a two-car garage, and a bedroom on the first floor."

*I hung up the phone and looked around. The thought of sorting and packing so much stuff was over-whelming. It's the only time in the whole process that I had second thoughts.*

"What's your budget?"

"I'd like to stay around $250,000 and pay cash from the equity in my house. My goal is to get rid of my house payment and the cost of upkeep here and be able to retire whenever I'm ready. Do you have anything I can look at now?"

Long silence. "Unfortunately, the market is at a standstill right now. I have clients waiting and no properties to show them. But I'll do some research, see what I can find, and get back to you."

I hung up the phone and looked around. That's the only time in the whole moving process that I had second thoughts. I was living in a beautiful, four-bedroom home, complete with a family room with vaulted ceiling and fireplace; a den with a wood stove and built-in bookcases; a huge living room, a dining room, an eat-in kitchen; a carport; a whole-house generator which gave me power in our numerous storms; and a tree-shaded deck overlooking two wooded acres that included a two-car detached garage and three large storage buildings – all full!

I confess I got a little panicky at that point. But I reminded myself of the time and money involved in the upkeep of all this wonderfulness. I also visualized what it would be like to be debt-free, retired, and able to sit down and write poetry any time inspiration struck. The vision won. I never looked back.

# The Purge

Chelle called me back that same day to tell me there was nothing in my price range or even higher, but she would keep looking. I guess I shouldn't have been surprised after our first conversation, but I was, and disappointed. Now that I had made this momentous decision, I wanted to move on it immediately. She also said she would send out letters to all the residents of Shannon's community, requesting they get in touch if they wanted to sell their house, and adding the incentive of a cash sale. We crossed our fingers.

She had told me earlier that she felt my house would sell quickly, maybe even the first day. I knew we couldn't list it until I had someplace to go. I told her in the beginning, I didn't want to risk having to put my stuff in storage and move into a temporary space. Not an option. That meant I had to be patient. I kept remembering my friend, Jeannie's favorite phrase, "Give me patience and give it to me right now."

*Living small and lean was not one of my husband's virtues. He lived by the mantra — "If one item is good, then five of that item is even better."*

Downsizing from a large house to a much smaller one is always challenging, but it was even more so in my case. My amazing husband had many virtues. Living small and lean was not one of them. He lived by the mantra – "If one item is good, then five of that item is even better." When he died, and I had to clean out his garage, I was forced to admit, the man was a hoarder, extraordinaire!

At that time, there was barely a path from the front to the back of that garage. We had to start with a small corner in the front and work our way through. In the middle of my grief, I spent weeks, along with his two best buddies, Charlie and Al, clearing out that building. I became convinced that screwdrivers must somehow have figured out how to clone themselves and multiply. I stopped counting at a hundred.

We were puzzled by many of the things he had saved – boxes of worn-out windshield wipers and battery cables; buckets full of screws, nails, and broken pieces of things; tools that didn't work; tools that had never been taken out of the boxes; mystery tools none of us could identify; even car engines and old tires. I had no idea how to price things for the yard sales.

Another of Don's friends, Paul, is a mechanic. He came over and helped me figure out prices and stayed with me through three yard sales. By then, I didn't care whether they paid me or not. I just wanted the stuff gone! We donated truckloads to Habitat for Humanity and hauled at least six more truckloads to the dump. By the time we had cleared the floor, I was so sick of it that I decreed we'd tackle the workbenches and shelves later. I couldn't face another day. Well, later never came.

Fast forward ten years. Since there were no houses to tour, I decided to begin what I would call, *The Great Purge*. I thought the garage should be the first area cleaned out, before summer's heat made it miserable. Don's two loyal friends from the first clean-out were ten years older with health issues. I knew I couldn't call on them again. Fortunately, I have a wonderful team of two brothers, Chris and Terry, plus Chris' son, Christopher, who maintain my lawn and do house repairs for me. They agreed to help.

We dived in. A couple of days and a dump run later, we still had so many tools and miscellaneous stuff, a round of yard sales seemed the most logical solution. Chris brought in saw horses and plywood to set up two rows of large tables in the clean garage. I borrowed a couple of fold-up tables to create a third row. We covered everything with red plastic tablecloths from Dollar Tree and started filling the tables. We were in business!

*I would sort and purge the storage buildings and house during the week, and my daughter, Shannon, would come on week-ends and carry the saleable items out to our red-draped tables. When they were full, we'd schedule a Saturday sale.*

Over the years, as Don had filled the garage, his treasures spilled over into three other large storage buildings. Those were not as horrendous as the garage. You could walk through them. But they required days of sorting, trashing, and donating. He had turned one storage building into a framing workshop, and it housed hundreds of frames, all shapes and sizes. Habitat inherited all those, but as usual, even that wasn't simple. We discovered the local ant community had built a winter retreat in there. It took several cans of spray to convince them to leave. Also, a lizard had moved in with them and the floor was littered with glops of poop that had to be cleaned up.

9

I would sort and purge the storage buildings and house during the week, and my daughter, Shannon, would come on week-ends and carry the saleable items out to our red-draped tables. When they were full, we'd schedule a Saturday sale. The following Monday, Habitat would collect the leftovers, and we'd start over. You get the picture. I dreaded the first sale, but each one turned out to be fun, even enlightening. I met new neighbors. My friends came and stayed to visit between customers, who, to my surprise, were talkative and shared interesting stories. One of my friends, Corliss, found an album by one of her teenage idols, Tommy Sands, that triggered a hilarious tale about her stalking him after a concert, back in the day. Even the shoppers listened and laughed.

There were also serendipitous moments. One of the items going away was an antique brass postal scale, complete with tiny individual weights stored in hand-made wooden boxes. I feared it would not find a home, but one day, I was explaining to a shopper what it was, and her face lit up. Turned out, she was a longtime postal employee and was delighted to carry home a piece of history. I knew Don would be so happy someone else would love his treasure.

We also had a fun surprise one Saturday when Santa came to visit, long white beard and all! He was in shorts instead of his red suit, but his jolly smile and twinkling eyes made it easy to see why he was chosen to portray Father Christmas in Colonial Williamsburg. Mrs. Santa explained they had been playing the famous couple for many years and shared some of the fun experiences they had enjoyed. "During covid," they said, "Santa still showed up but wearing a clear face shield and talking to the children from a short distance, instead of on his lap"

We quickly developed a routine. Chris came to the first sale to help me price and sell the tools. After that, it was just Shannon and me. She would come at 7:30 and put the signs out by the main road and in the neighborhood. We'd block off the driveway. Shoppers would park on the street and walk back to the detached garage. There was some whining, mostly from people who looked like they actually needed the exercise. But generally, people were good-natured about the short hike. We lucked out with the weather each time. It was cool and sunny, and people seemed genuinely excited to be outdoors on a pretty, spring day.

Sales started at 8. Sometimes, over-eager shoppers would arrive early and park in front of the house, but most of them would wait politely till the doors opened at 8. We discovered a pattern of steady shoppers till about 11, when it would slow down a little. I would make sandwiches and we would picnic during the lull. The menu also became routine – cheese slices on buns with dill pickles, garlic spread, and mayo. Sometimes, I threw in potato chips for a treat. It was the perfect "eat fast, no clean up" snack.

One day, after lunch, an attractive grey-haired lady came and introduced herself as the Jewelry Lady. She told us she buys glitzy jewelry and markets it in New York, where, she explained, "The women really love sparkle." It was another of those serendipitous moments. I am a jewelry junkie. I have enough earrings to start my own store. A lot of them are glitzy, because that's what Mary Kay Directors wear – the bigger, the better! I had been wondering what to do with my large stash.

She also told us she buys Native American jewelry. My years of attending powwows and wandering the Southwest with Don, resulted in a stunning collection of unique silver and gemstone jewelry. He loved buying me gifts and gave me jewelry for special occasions, plus "I love you" gifts for no reason at all. I decided Shannon and I would go through the collection, choose the things we knew we would wear, and the rest could be sold to help fund the move. Our sales lasted till 2 p.m., when we would take down the signs, pack up the boxes for Habitat, close the garage doors, put our feet up, and count our loot. We were a well-oiled machine! The four sales contributed nearly $800 to the moving fund. I thought that was pretty good, considering a few items were $5, but most were $1 - $3.

*I had put my foot down when Don and I moved in together after many years of separate houses. I was determined our house together would not look like his previous hoarder houses. He cooperated, except for the walls. He wasn't happy unless every inch of the wall was covered with a piece of art.*

# THE CHOICES

Clearing out the garage and storage buildings was relatively painless. Most everything needed to go – either to the dump, Habitat, or a thrift store. I didn't have to ask that controversial question, "Does this give me joy?" When I started on the house, it was an entirely different situation. In the downsizing, I would be losing a den, a family room, a bedroom, which doubled as my Mary Kay room, and two medium-sized storage rooms, all filled with furniture and stuff.

I had put my foot down when Don and I moved in together after many years of separate houses. I was determined our house together would not look like his previous hoarder houses. He cooperated, except for the walls. He wasn't happy unless every inch of the wall was covered with a piece of art.

Our compromise was, hands off the living room, dining room, our bedroom and my office. I would select the furnishings for those. The large, vaulted-ceiling family room became a museum for all the unique Native American art pieces we had collected during twenty-five years of traveling in the Southwest. It was filled with pottery, kachinas, paintings, prints, baskets, dream-catchers, and Don's large collection of carved bears – all sizes and types. There was also an entire wall of bookcases, filled with our favorite reading material, photos, and more Indian art. At the time, as we were building this collection, I rationalized it was classy hoarding.

The den housed an antique desk, built-in bookshelves filled with beautiful coffee table books, travel guides, and more photos. Photography was one of Don's retirement hobbies. He took photos constantly on our trips. When we returned home, I converted them into colorful scrapbooks that filled the cabinets. His walls were covered with interesting prints and one-of-a-kind clay and feathered masks, created by a Cherokee artist we met at a powwow. My ancestry is Cherokee, so they were especially meaningful.

*How could I choose what to keep and what would have to go? All the interesting colleticles brought me joy.*

Don had spent thirty-one years traveling the world in the Air Force before I met him. There were dozens of other interesting collectibles, or as I sometimes called them, dustibles, scattered around the house. They all brought me joy.

How could I choose what to keep and what would have to go? The pain began.

# The Search

Since Chelle had nothing to show me, I decided to check out some of the townhouse communities around town on my own, driving through and making notes of the ones I liked. I really wanted to be in Shannon's neighborhood but I also realized that might not happen, so I needed a Plan B. Many of the places I visited were concrete jungles with several two or three-story buildings jammed together, side-by-side and back-to-back, with little or no green space. They felt suffocating after my wooded oasis. Shannon started searching Zillow, and we would compare notes during our daily evening chats.

About two weeks after the decision to move, Chelle called with two properties available. Both had garages, a bedroom on the first floor and two more upstairs. One was $370,000 and one was $350,000. Our searches on Zillow had brought us to the conclusion that I probably wasn't going to find what I needed for less than $350,000. At that level, I could pay off the mortgage of $158,000 and still have enough cash for the new place from the estimated proceeds, probably $500,000 - $550,00. That would leave enough to pay movers and miscellaneous expenses without dipping into savings. The numbers were constantly running through my brain.

Could I really pull this off?

I was excited to start the search. The houses were on opposite sides of town but only about fifteen minutes from Shannon. The first one was in one of those concrete jungles. It had a garage in front and a dark side entrance. The interior was shocking. The people were still living in the house and hadn't bothered to straighten up. Clutter was everywhere, and a dog was barking at us from a large cage by the entrance.

*The interior was shocking. The people were still living in the house and hadn't bothered to straighten up. "Picture it empty," my realtor said. Yikes!*

My impulse was to leave immediately but we fought our way through the debris with Chelle saying, "Picture it empty." Not so easy. The stairs creaked badly. The carpet would have to be replaced, and the rooms were dark, without much natural light. The tiny balcony overlooking another building, wasn't even big enough for a chair. Nothing green anywhere. Didn't require any thought. It was a No! The eye-opener for me was learning later that it sold for over the asking price that same day with several offers.

The second house was just the opposite. It was in an older community with trees and flowers. The house had been updated with new appliances, carpet, paint. It had three bedrooms with a master suite downstairs and a large loft room upstairs that would be perfect for my bookcases and native art. The vaulted ceilings and tall windows made it bright and cheerful. There was a small, grassless, fenced yard with a covered patio. I immediately envisioned an Arizona-type yard with rocks and native plantings. I could see myself living happily in this house. We made an offer. I waited and hoped. The next day, we learned there had been many offers and it sold for way over the asking price of $370,000. I was disappointed, but my philosophical friend, Vivien, insisted there was something better for me out there. She repeated my own favorite saying back to me, "Onward and upward!"

*I could manage the price if I took some money from my retirement fund. Should I bite the bullet and commit? The next morning, the cautious voice inside my head said, "No, keep looking."*

A couple of days later, I noticed a listing for a new townhouse community about ten minutes west of town. Chelle hadn't called me about it because it was over my budget at $400,000. Also, I really didn't want to be farther out of town, but I decided it would be worth looking at the model for comparison. It supposedly had everything I wanted – the downstairs bedroom, two-car garage and it was new. That was a big plus. I wouldn't have to worry about appliances dying or heat pumps going down. Shannon went with me. When we got there, we were surprised to see a dusty field with survey stakes -- not even a model home to walk through. The realtor showed us floor plans and sample materials for floors, appliances, etc. The houses wouldn't be available until October, but they were already almost sold out.

Chelle drove us out to look at one of the two building sites left, and I tried to picture a future home there. At least they weren't back-to-back like some of the other communities I'd seen.

There would be green space between buildings, and the entire area was surrounded by trees. But $400,000 was a long way from the $250,000 I'd originally planned to spend. That night, I went over the drawings with the room sizes and measured my current ones for comparison. I could make it work, and I could manage the price if I took some money from my retirement fund. Should I bite the bullet and commit? The next morning, the cautious voice inside my head said, "No, keep looking."

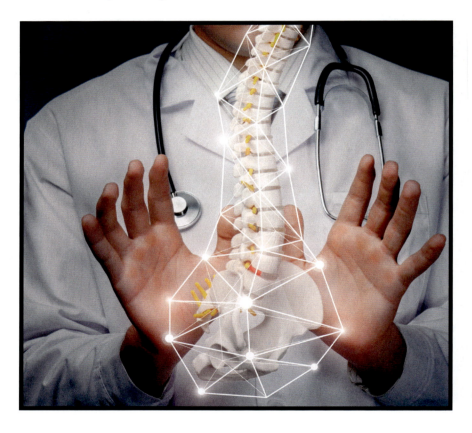

*My back issues were already limiting, and my scoliosis and spinal stenosis would continue to worsen, I was sure, despite the best efforts of my chiropractor to keep me walking. Surgery was not an option, so adapting and learning to manage the disability was my only choice.*

A month had gone by. We were into June, and still, no house. Several of my friends had downsized and moved to a beautiful over-55 community called Villas at Five Forks. It was convenient, near all my doctors and my usual shopping areas, which would be important if driving became more difficult. My back issues were already limiting, and my scoliosis and spinal stenosis would continue to worsen, I was sure, despite the best efforts of my chiropractor to keep me walking. Surgery was not an option, so adapting and learning to manage the disability was my only choice. The Villas were perfect because everything was on the first floor, unlike all the other townhomes I'd seen. They had a unit with three bedrooms, a den which could be my library for the bookcases and art, and a two-car garage. There was nothing for sale at the moment, but I reasoned – it's a retirement community, and people's circumstances change, so, maybe something would open up.

In the meantime, I called my friend, Cindy, who moved there a couple of years ago, explained my search, and she invited me out for a tour of her home. I fell in love with the house. It was bright, the rooms were big, and it was beautifully finished. Combine that with the wooded surroundings, walking trails, and a clubhouse with a pool, and it seemed like a great place to live. A *Sweet Adeline* chorus friend from years ago, Donna, also lived there, so I'd have my very own support system in my new place. There were two big downers. The homeowners' fee was $450 a month and the houses started at $400,000 but would probably go to $450,000 or more in a bidding contest. The neighborhood was much in demand, and Cindy told me realtors were constantly knocking on doors, hoping for an available unit.

I spent the evening doing the numbers. I could do as much as $450,000 and still be able to pay cash. Early in the process, I'd applied for and received a $105,000 home equity loan, just in case I wound up in a situation like this. I reasoned that my house would also probably have more than one offer and sell for more than we planned to ask. I could then restore my savings and pay off the equity loan at closing. It was risky, but this particular housing opportunity seemed worth the risk. It had everything I needed and wanted. The next morning, I called Cindy and asked her to put a note on the bulletin board at the clubhouse with my name and phone number, asking if anyone was interested in selling their house for a fast cash payment. I took a deep breath and waited.

I felt relieved that I'd made a decision and could now focus on the other stressful happening in my life. Mary Kay Sales Directors can earn a company car every two years. My group of eighty-one beautiful ladies, called Sharon's Shining Stars, was in that six-month qualification period for car #23. June was our last month, and it was proving to be the most difficult one yet. I needed to stop worrying about houses and move on to cars.

Then the phone rang. It was Chelle.

# The Surprise

"I got a call this morning from a homeowner in Williamsburg Village at Norge, responding to the letters we sent out. She has an end unit with a two-car garage, three bedrooms, master suite on the first floor, and large loft room. It's 2,460 sq. ft. and she's asking $300,000, way under what it's worth. The only bad thing is, she won't be ready to move for four to six months. She says it will take her that long to pack up because she has a fulltime job."

I was shocked, I didn't know what to say. I had given up hope of finding something there. It had been over a month since the letters went out, and we'd had no response. I remember muttering something about not being able to wait that long and reminding her that I had decided to wait for a house in the Villas.

"But this is where you really wanted to be and the price is amazing. Don't you want to look at it?"

Sanity prevailed, finally. "Yes, of course, let's look at it. Nothing to lose. But it sounds too good to be true."

I couldn't have been more wrong. It was everything I wanted. The rooms were big, with tall windows and lots of light. The vaulted ceiling loft room would be perfect for my tall bookcases. I had anticipated I would probably have to paint and re-carpet whatever I bought, but this place was immaculate – walls, carpet, everything. It had a little patio in the back with a grassy hill and trees that made it private and cozy.

My only concern was the steep stairs up to the office, guest room and loft. But, I had considered getting a stair lift for my present house. I could do that here. With the price at $300,000, there would be enough money to cover it. Chelle reminded me that the price was firm because there was no other realtor involved. The homeowners had come directly to us. I wouldn't get shafted again in a bidding war. And, it was $100,000 - $150,000 less than the Villas. Before we left 301 Kinde Circle, I had already decided I wanted to live there.

Chelle drew up the contract that evening and left a message for the homeowners, who I learned were a mother and adult daughter. We offered the $300,000 asking price. To make the offer more enticing, we added an extra $5000 for packing and moving expenses if they would vacate by August 1, instead of four to six months down the road. They didn't respond to Chelle's phone message for a couple of days. I couldn't figure out why they wouldn't want to know immediately what our offer was. The strangeness would continue through our negotiations.

When they finally did call back, they didn't want to hear the offer over the phone. They wanted to sit down with Chelle at her office. A meeting was scheduled in two days. I was a nervous wreck but trying to hold it together and focus on my Mary Kay car qualification. The meeting day arrived, and they cancelled, saying something had come up. They rescheduled for three days later. We waited impatiently. They cancelled again, this time explaining that the mother was ill. Chelle offered again to go over the offer by phone. The response was a hard, "No!"

Finally, the meeting happened. Chelle called to say the daughter was really excited about the moving money. The mother sat stone-faced and didn't respond at all. They both seemed surprised we had offered them the asking price. It was obvious they didn't realize the price was about $65,000 under the market value. They insisted they needed to think about the offer. This was a Tuesday. They called later to ask if we would give them until Saturday. They planned to leave the next day to go to Tennessee to look for a house. We were encouraged. Now, if they could just find one...and what if they didn't? Would that shoot down the whole deal?

It was a long, long time from Wednesday to Saturday. I stayed busy getting ready for our last yard sale. We had decided everything left over would get packed up for Habitat, and the tables taken down so the garage would be empty when we put the house on the market. We were getting ready to move into the next phase of this crazy process. Saturday turned out to be our best sale yet. We had lots of people and over $300 in sales. I kept checking my phone and texting Chelle, hoping for news. It didn't come until late in the afternoon.

"They said yes and agreed to vacate by August 1." Shannon and I were ecstatic. This was  going to happen

*When I received the inspector's report - thirty-five pages - he reassured me it was rare to find so few things wrong. Would the sellers fix the issues, or did I need to add it to my list of expenses?*

# The Inspection

The next step was the home inspection. I was surprised to learn I would be able to be there and even more surprised when Chele said it would take about three hours. She explained that would give me some time to look around the house, take measurements, etc. Shannon took a little time from work and joined us, seeing the house for the first time. She thought it was beautiful and, like us, was blown away by the size of the rooms. Her house is a two-bedroom model, so she had never actually seen one of the end units, which are much larger. She measured the rooms and took pictures so I could figure out where to place furniture, etc. Big decisions were ahead about which items would go with me and what would have to be sold or donated.

Our sellers had already been packing, so the whole downstairs was filled with boxes and bins with barely a path from room to room. When I saw that, I became concerned about what the carpet was going to look like when those heavy containers were removed. I wondered if I might have to replace it in the living room and dining room. One more expense.

When I received the inspector's thirty-five-page report the next day, I was relieved to see he had found very few problems. The ice-maker and water dispenser didn't work; an earlier air handler leak in the attic had left some stains on the walls and ceilings; the strip along the bottom of the shower door needed to be replaced; the electrical outlet on the patio didn't work, and the electrical element in the fireplace seemed to be malfunctioning. That was it. He reassured me it was rare to find so few things wrong. It was a win!

Chelle went through the whole reluctant appointment-setting thing again with the homeowners and finally was able to meet with them three days later to go over the report. I was disappointed but not surprised to learn they refused to do any of the repairs. I would have to add that to my list of expenses, which would include the stairlift.

# The Stairlift

After a lot of research and a long conversation with my friends, John and Penny, who had purchased one themselves, I narrowed the list down to two possibilities – Bruno, their choice, and Nautilus.

I learned, because my staircase was curved, the lift would have to be custom-built, which could take from six weeks to three months. The prospect of navigating those steep stairs for a prolonged period of time was daunting. So was the price – probably $5000 to $10,000. But, I reminded myself, there really was no choice. I had to do this. I made appointments for the estimates as soon as the representatives could schedule them and called Chelle to make the arrangements with the homeowners. Again, resistance. They didn't want anyone in the house. Chelle explained the importance of expediency, that I wouldn't be able to navigate the steep stairs safely. They finally agreed to let us in for two hours on the scheduled date. I would meet with one representative at 2 p.m. and the other at 3 p.m. Onward!

While Connor, the first rep, was measuring and taking photos, I had a second opportunity to confirm some of my measurements and try to figure out furniture placement. The downstairs rooms - living room, dining room, kitchen, and master bedroom were smaller than my current ones, so it was like putting together a puzzle with pieces that didn't quite fit. The plus side of that first-floor reality was the fact that the two-car garage would allow me to keep the shelves in my storage building and most of the things I had stored on them. It was a trade-off.

When Connor finished his complicated calculations, he showed me on the computer exactly how the system would be built, from steel, with a lifetime guarantee on the parts and little, if any, maintenance.

There would be a control at both the top and bottom of the stairs, so I would be able to move the lift as needed from either floor. Because of the space limitations downstairs, I was going to have to store my Mary Kay product in my office on the second floor, so that meant getting boxes of product up the stairs. I could now see that would be simple. I'd just put them and myself on the lift, and up we'd go! Good news.

The price news was not as good -- $15,000 to $18,000. I was shocked! He promised to get an exact price, with contract to me the next day. Obviously, the sooner I could make a decision and get the process started, the sooner I could have the lift. Again, he estimated four to six weeks.

Representative #2, John, arrived eagerly early with a piece of steel and a piece of something that looked like plastic. Their lifts were built from the latter, which he insisted required less maintenance than the steel models. He looked at the curved stairs and explained that he installed only the straight stairlifts but would have one of his colleagues contact me with more information. That person wasn't available for my appointment, so John was filling in. He estimated, without taking any measurements, the lift could cost as much as $14,000. I thanked him and sent him on his way. I never heard from him or his colleague again.

When Connor got in touch the next day, as promised, with a price of $15,880 for the Bruno Elite, I swallowed hard and signed the contract. Shannon and I decided a machine that exclusive, needed a personalized name. She said, "Think of it as being carried up the stairs in the arms of a handsome man." I immediately chose Magic Mike. I should point out that naming my appliances was not a new thing. I had also named the Robo vacuum she gave me for my birthday. Elvis now rocks and rolls all over my floors.

# THE MOVER

*Pack - Move - Budget*
*Can we do it?*

With the stairlift decision pinned down, the next task was to find a mover. Chelle recommended a company she'd worked with many times and found to be dependable and reasonably priced. After the financial blow of the stairlift, that was important, so I called and set up an appointment. Meanwhile, I was continuing to purge every nook and cranny of my house. I worked on it every day between Mary Kay chores, making piles of Trash, Donate, and ????, which Shannon carried away each Saturday. I was so grateful for her strong arms and legs to do what I couldn't and so appreciative of her sunny willingness to do anything she could to help, including ordering dinner for me on busy days. The work was grueling, but like the yard sales, we made it fun.

Austin arrived on time for our appointment, looking like he was fresh out of college, but disarming me with his knowledge and experience at this moving game. As we toured the house, he took constant notes on his phone, asking questions and answering all of mine. I explained that some of the excess furniture was going to be adopted by Shannon. Since she lived in the same neighborhood, could it get delivered the same day he moved my belongings? The answer was, "Yes." I was sold.

I had decided at the very beginning of this adventure, that I couldn't possibly pack everything myself. I would want them to pack and, also, do some unpacking. Austin showed me how they calculate the price of a move. It's based on the number of people needed; the hours required to pack, move, and unpack; the number of trucks required; the distance, plus extra for any items requiring special attention, like my grandfather clock. I had budgeted $10,000 for the move but hoped it might be less. His detailed, itemized estimate arrived the next day -- $10,736.27. I signed the contract.

We set the packing days for August 16 and 17, with moving days of August 18 and 19. Unpacking would occur on August 20. I breathed a little easier. Every decision made, every unneeded item removed from the house, made me feel lighter and freer.

# THE CAR

That last week in June was also the deadline for our every-two-year car re-qualification. We needed twelve more consultants to place Mary Kay orders by Friday, June 30, at 9 p.m. I was on the phone and computer all week, trying to line up those orders. It was a discouraging process with lots of "no's." I wasn't at all sure we could do it. But I kept plugging away. Attaining car status meant an additional $450 a month in income for two years or the use of a new, leased car for that same length of time. In the last few years, I have chosen the money option. By Thursday, we were down to six orders. Progress! By Friday, we still needed three. I could see light at the end of this six-month-long tunnel. By noon, our $45,000 sales requirement had been met, and car #23 was a reality! Happy dance!!! Now, I could focus entirely on the move.

*"Did you know there's a dead woodpecker in your carport?"*

# THE WOODPECKER

July 1 started the countdown to the sale of my house, which would begin July 15. Chelle was cautiously optimistic that it would sell quickly, maybe even the first day. Two others in the neighborhood had sold recently – one over the asking price of $500,000 and the other for slightly under that same asking price of $500,000. Both houses were smaller than mine, without the added features of three large storage buildings, a two-car detached garage, an all-house generator, a fireplace and a wood stove. They each had several offers the first day.

Shannon and I still had lots of work to do. It was time to temporarily stop the purging and concentrate on packing up photos, what nots from table tops, and make the house look as if no one lived there. I understood the philosophy of prospective homeowners being able to see themselves living in the house without the distraction of someone else's personal belongings, but it was a big job.

The family room with the Native American art collection was the hardest. It was impossible to clear everything, but I did manage to declutter the wall of bookcases, the fireplace hearth, and table tops. The curio cabinets would have to remain as is. I had a plan for them but couldn't execute it before Chelle started showing the house. Son, Steven, who lives in Kentucky, had escaped the whole cleaning-out process because of distance, his multiple jobs, three kids, and the busyness that goes along with all that. But we had made plans for him to come home for a short visit, and we would divide the art collection between the three of us, each choosing their favorites. We finished that room first and moved on to the rest of the house.

We had started working on the Mary Kay room/bedroom that first Saturday in July when my carpenter, Terry, arrived to do some small repairs.

"Did you know there's a dead woodpecker on your carport?"

I was horrified. When you live in the woods, dead things sometimes appear because of Mother Nature's grand scheme of things, but I had never gotten used to it.

"Are you sure it's dead?"

"It didn't move when I nudged it."

I knew what to do. Reluctantly, I called my neighbor, Bob. He is my all-around rescuer. When I found the black snake in my living room, he caught it and carried it to the woods, refusing to kill it. He had also buried a myriad of small critters, insisting they deserved a proper ending. He had buried a bird just last week that had committed involuntary suicide by slamming into my sliding glass door. He came over right away with his shovel, but we couldn't find the bird. I was relieved. Maybe it had just been stunned, had recovered and flown away. Then Shannon spotted something farther down the driveway.

"Isn't that a woodpecker?"

When Bob approached, it didn't fly away. Strangely, it hopped toward him, stopped by his foot, and just looked up at him. When Bob moved, the bird followed, as if to say, "Help!" It was obviously injured, was hopping on one foot and its wings looked damaged. Bob's next-door neighbor, Julie, does animal rescue, so we called her. She was out on a mission, but luckily, a friend who works with her was there and came over. She recognized the woodpecker as one they had raised from a fledgling and released just a couple of days earlier. Apparently, he wasn't quite ready for the wilds, so back he went, to the hospital cage in Julie's yard. Bob and his shovel went happily home, and Shannon and I continued our chores.

# THE TRIP DOWN MEMORY LANE

This entire cleaning-out process was an abbreviated journey back through my life. I decided to steal the title of one of my favorite movies and call it Back to the Future. I have always saved things like special notes, cards, photos. While going through an old trunk that hadn't been opened in years, I found scrapbooks with yellowed newspaper clippings and memorabilia from high school, college, and my first job as an executive secretary in the office of the governor of West Virginia. As I cleaned out my office, I tunneled through forty years of Mary Kay awards, ribbons, photos of meetings around the country.

It all brought back memories of people who were important to me at different times in my life, but I hadn't thought of in years. We had lost touch, and I now wondered what had happened to them. Were they still alive or gone like so many friends and family members. As we get older, we begin to feel like the unicorn – the last one of our kind. The items also reminded me of how fortunate I had been to have people come into my life at times when I really needed them for support and guidance or to be partners in fun adventures. What to do with those souvenirs from the past?

As the pile of discards grew, I began to wonder if I'd been suffering for a long time from a mild case of PTSD. It wasn't just the upkeep of the house itself that burdened me. It was also this old stuff, tucked away in trunks and drawers, waiting to be dumped on my children when I was no longer able to make decisions for myself. The problem had haunted me, but I couldn't decide how to resolve it. It had seemed an impossible task. Now that I realized I didn't have to keep the stuff to keep the memories, I felt lighter and happier as stack after stack went away.

*After my husband's death, I spent time clearing out his desk, finding important papers, and clearing stuff that oozed from every drawer. the memories made it much harder than I expected.*

# The Den

After Don's death in 2013, I spent days going through his huge, old-fashioned desk to find important papers and clear out debris that oozed from every drawer. I had written a poem about all the nostalgic, funny things I found. I had left the bookcases as is, filled with photos, collectibles and lots of books. I needed to now tackle that whole room and depersonalize as much as possible.

It was much harder than I expected. The travel books reminded me of the many interesting places we'd been, and the photos brought Don back to me so clearly. Old notes in his handwriting also brought back the pain of his loss. But I was determined to muddle through, trying as I had when he died, to focus on the happy days. Leaving our house would, in a way, be leaving him, but I knew nothing could ever take away the memories. At the end of the day, I was proud of the way the room looked and, more importantly, I was at peace with the memories.

Another big challenge resolved itself that evening. When Don's mom, Martha, passed, he traveled home to Kansas City for the funeral and to empty out her house, with the help of his brother, Dave, and Dave's daughter, Teresa. He rented a U-Haul and brought back several pieces of furniture, which we would later move into our present house. Some of those pieces would go with me to my new place, but some, unfortunately, would not fit.

Among those was the desk I'd just cleared; a massive antique campaign chest, circa 1790; five elaborately carved wooden wall clocks, from Germany and Austria; and some of Martha's artwork. She was a talented painter, potter, and crafter. I wanted those things to stay in the family. Don's only sibling, Dave, and his wife had both died years ago, but Teresa and I had stayed in touch, becoming close over the years.

She and husband, Larry, had come to visit me many times, so when I called and described the pieces I couldn't take with me, she knew immediately what they were. Even better, she said she would love to have them and would share with her kids and grandkids. She might even be interested in the large teak table that wouldn't fit in my small kitchen. She'd do some research to figure out the logistics of getting them moved in the next few days. I told her I knew Don would be so happy they would be enjoyed by another Frew generation. I collapsed in my chair and breathed a sigh of relief. Again, onward!

# The Count-Down

## *The Second Purge*

It was one week before Chelle would start showing the house. My to-do list was still long. Chris and son, Christopher, came on Monday, determined to work as long as it took to clear the last of the junk from the garage and make the lawn look as perfect as possible. It was one of our hottest days, and unbearably humid. We were soaking wet with sweat. But we persevered and by four o'clock, the lawn was mowed and trimmed, the storage building was cleared of lizard droppings, and the garage was purged of all traces of Don's hoarding.

In the middle of the day, house cleaners came to give the house that extra sparkle that I wasn't able to do – vacuuming, bathroom cleaning, floor mopping, dusting, etc. At least that was the plan. A group of three young Latina ladies arrived on time and attacked the upstairs like a swarm of bees. An hour later, they packed up their buckets and brooms and left, explaining that a second crew would clean the downstairs.

Part B didn't go so well. Nobody spoke English, and the boss had not arrived to tell them what to do. I tried to explain with gestures, but they just stared at me, smiled pleasantly, and proceeded to do what they chose. Some unnecessary things were done, and other important things were not. Consequently, I wound up scrubbing the kitchen floor, waxing the wood floor in the dining room, and cleaning all the mirrors and glass doors myself. Plus, as they dusted, they moved things and didn't put anything back where it belonged.

When they left, I went back out to the garage. I still couldn't believe the guys were actually able to accomplish all that in a day. We were all too tired to celebrate, but it was an amazing feeling to be done. I wandered out to the garage again before dark, just to reassure myself that it was empty and clean.

I had one day left to make sure each room was as pristine and neutral as possible for the photographer to capture all the wonderfulness of the house on Wednesday. No family pictures; table tops and counters cleared; fresh flowers on the dining room and kitchen tables. It needed to look as if nobody lived here. Mission accomplished! The pics were lovely. Who could resist this great house!

I spent Thursday trying to catch up on my life, my Mary Kay business, and some earlier-than-midnight sleep.

## THE SHOWINGS

The house "went live," as Chelle described it, on Friday. She scheduled an appointment at 12:30 and one at 1:30. One was a family who had driven up from Florida, hoping to find a house and get moved before school started. Chelle asked if I could be out a week early, and after thinking it through, I decided I could. I hibernated at Shannon's while the showings were going on. We heard nothing that night from either client. The next showing was Saturday at 10. I was disappointed so few appointments had been booked. Chele admitted she was surprised too. I had been so sure we would have lots of interest, and everyone had predicted the house would sell by the end of the week-end. Now I was worried.

As week one ended with several showings and no offers, I obviously had to revise my assumptions that the house would sell quickly, to the more realistic – the house will sell. Chelle kept reassuring me, "It only takes one." Where was that one?

Meanwhile, the purging continued. Shannon came for our usual Saturday clean out and carried out the things I couldn't manage myself. About 2 p.m., she headed out with her car full of donations to the library and thrift store, only to be waylaid by bumper-to-bumper traffic that resulted in a fender-bender. Thank goodness, she was all right, but the front of her car was damaged, and that would complicate our lives. What a bummer! I felt so bad for her. It didn't seem fair to have to deal with that while in the middle of a good deed! Bah humbug!

The incident did not turn out well. The insurance company totaled her old car, and she was forced to shop for another, which meant taking on car payments she had been hoping to avoid for a few more months. With her van out of commission, our carry-out system came to a temporary halt. She would eventually find the Honda model she wanted, and we were back in business, but there were several days of confusion and stress in between.

As week three of our showings began with zero offers, I had a brief bout of panic. On Tuesday, August 1, I'd be closing on the new house and handing over a check that would practically empty my retirement account. I'd already had to pay up front for 75% of the cost of the stair lift. In two weeks, I'd have to write a hefty check for the moving expense. I had made all those commitments based on the assumption that the house would sell quickly. The realization that it might not sell for weeks or even months, was terrifying.

Also, I had just learned that one of my friends who appeared to be perfectly healthy two months ago, had been diagnosed with terminal lung cancer – no cure, no treatment. My heart was broken that we would lose her. My concern for her triggered a chain of what-ifs. What if I had a stroke or fell or got sick or…the list went on. How would I pay for my care? My savings had always been my buffer against those what-ifs. Finally, I emerged from the fear fog and remembered the $105,000 equity loan I'd arranged at the beginning of this process, just in case the house didn't sell immediately and I needed emergency money. I breathed easier.

Meanwhile, the showings continued with some strange, unexpected results. On Chelle's advice, I had packed away valuables, thinking all the while, "Surely people won't bother my personal belongings." I was so wrong! After one showing, it was obvious someone had reclined on my guest bed. There was a full-body imprint on the bedspread. Another time, someone with very bad aim used the guest bathroom and left the mess. Ugh! After that, I cloroxed all the toilets after each showing.

I also noticed things on the tables would be in different places than I left them, indicating people were picking things up. "Where, " I asked Chelle, "was the realtor who was supposed to be in control?" She explained that some of them didn't want to risk offending the client by restraining them, so just let them do whatever they wanted. "Please," I begged my guardian angels, "let this process be over SOON!"

## THE CLOSING AND THE PAUSE

When I did the walk through for my new house, everything was immaculate. The carpets had some furniture indentations, but I figured my own furniture would cover most of that. It was my first time seeing it without all the boxes and bins. I was relieved that it looked bigger and able to accommodate most of the furniture I wanted to keep.

The garage was another story. At least twenty huge bags of trash filled one whole corner. The seller's explanation, "We were too tired to move them." Chelle stepped up and said she would pile them in her SUV and take them to the dump. Talk about above and beyond!

When I arrived at the title company office for the closing, I learned there had been more drama. The homeowners had balked at signing the final papers when they saw Chelle's commission listed, refusing to pay it, even though they had agreed to it in writing on the original sales contract. They said she had done nothing to earn it. I knew how many hours she had spent with them, patiently walking them through each step of the selling/moving process, even finding a mover for them. Their pettiness and animosity was hurtful to Chelle. Finally, after two heated hours of discussions, they signed the papers and stormed out.

My own signing and delivery of the check took all of ten minutes. The house was mine. I decided to go back by Kinde Circle on my way home. I just wanted to sit in the quiet house and claim it for my own. My friend, Kaye, who had set me on this path with her wise questioning, would come on Sunday with sage, and we would cleanse the house in my ancestral tradition.

Meanwhile, I had two weeks and lots more purging to do. We had decided to take my house off the market during that time so I could finish my chores without constant interruptions. Also, Chelle and many of the other realtors who had shown the house, felt it would be more saleable if it was empty. I hoped they were right.

## THE PIANO

As a little girl, I dreamed of having a piano and learning to play. My dad was a coal miner who worked long, hard hours in the mines for low pay. Extravagances like piano lessons were impossible, plus, where would we put a piano in our tiny house, even if we could afford it. When I grew up, married, and had children of my own, I was determined they would have the piano I had dreamed about. As a divorced mom, struggling to keep food on the table and a roof over our heads, a piano seemed as much out-of-reach as it was when I was a child. But I saved enough to buy an old upright, and was filled with joy when it arrived in our small living room. Let the lessons begin!

It's never a good idea to try to live vicariously through your children. Mine taught me that lesson. Steven was a fifer in the Colonial Williamsburg Fife and Drum Corps, so he already knew how to read music and found the lessons easier than Shannon, who was learning everything from the beginning. He would practice and make up little tunes of his own and did well at his recitals.

Shannon, on the other hand, had to be constantly reminded to practice and never sat down and played, just for the enjoyment of it. Finally, Sarah, her patient and very honest teacher, said, "Look, I can keep taking your money, but Shannon just isn't interested, and I don't think that's going to change." I suspect Shannon breathed a sigh of relief when I announced her lessons were cancelled. As for me, I used the kids' beginner books and taught myself a few of my favorite songs. My childhood dream finally came true.

When I saw the much smaller living room in my new house, I knew, sadly, the piano wouldn't make the furniture cut. Steven really wanted it, and for a brief shining moment, I pictured another generation of Dorsey kids sitting on that bench. Then reality intruded as I faced the fact that Adaline, Emma, and Zachary were runners, soccer, baseball, and basketball players. Sports was their thing, piano lessons, maybe, not so much. Steven, like me, also had a space-available issue, but he loved that old piano so much, he figured out a place to put it.

When the piano movers came, trundled it down the stairs, and headed off to Kentucky to make the magical delivery, I watched it go with mixed feelings. It was another transition in the long list of life changes. Feeling a little foolish, I thanked the piano for the joy it had brought me through forty-plus years and wished it many more years of musical service in its new home with the Steven Dorsey tribe. A chapter closed.

## THE PACKERS

They arrived together, a group of three smiling guys, apparently eager to box up all my belongings and carry them to my new home. They wasted no time in getting to the task. I showed them what needed to be done, they each chose a space and went to work. Shannon and I still had some fragile things that we wanted to pack ourselves, so we worked alongside them.

Austin, the owner of the moving company, had explained earlier that we were expected to provide lunch, drinks, and snacks, which I thought weird when I was paying him a fortune already, but we decided not to start off with a hungry crew. Every day of the packing and moving, Shannon made great sandwiches, and the guys would take a break when they needed it to munch on the goodies in the frig and on the table. They were very complimentary of the food. I hoped that goodwill would equate to fewer things broken or damaged. Didn't work out that way, but we tried.

The first day, I would jump every time I heard a clatter or bang in the kitchen or pantry, trying not to imagine the worst. By the second day, I was resigned to the ominous noises and just kept working instead of running to see what it was. Turned out, those two rooms came through pretty much intact, with just a couple of small things broken.

It was the quiet packer who did the most damage, packing heavy things on top of unwrapped lamp shades, resulting in total destruction, and putting a glass seashell lamp in the bottom of a huge box, unwrapped, with heavy things on top. Sadly, it didn't survive. By 3 p.m. on the second day, I was happy to see all of them go, not realizing the same crew would be back the next day to move all the things they'd just packed.

## THE MOVING

The two moving days were utter chaos. Six men were constantly in and out-carrying furniture that had been bubble-wrapped, boxes of all sizes, and continuing to pack last-minute things like pictures and breakables. They decided to move the furniture that was going to Shannon's house first in a smaller truck with a couple of guys, while the rest packed the big truck with my stuff. At first, out of curiosity, I watched things going into the truck, but after seeing them stack heavy boxes on top of my coffee table and turn my dresser on its end, I couldn't take it. I stayed inside and began packing the leftover breakables myself. It was a wise move. Everything Shannon and I packed arrived intact.

When the truck was all packed and ready to go, Shannon and I rushed over to Kinde Circle and tried to guide things to the right rooms on the right floor. She stayed upstairs, and I did the downstairs. We'd gone over and over where everything was to go, but there was still some confusion because they were moving things in so quickly.

The living room and dining room quickly filled up with stacked boxes. We had managed to get the furniture mostly in place with the rows of boxes down the middle. Soon, the kitchen and pantry were full of boxes too. I kept wondering how there could be so many boxes when we had already purged so much. Finally, the truck was empty, the guys grabbed one last sandwich and were gone. We had survived Day 1.

We locked the doors and went back to the Tanbark house to survey the territory. Most everything from downstairs was gone except my chair and the entertainment center. I had requested they leave those until Day 2. I knew I'd need some distraction after the wild day. The furniture that was being donated to friends and family would wait for pick up until everything else was moved. The next day, the upstairs would be moved. I spent my last night in my old home, watching TV in a nearly empty living room and sleeping in my bedroom, surrounded by boxes. I was too tired to care how bizarre it all was.

Day 2 was a repeat of Day 1, but on steroids. Shannon and I packed more breakables. The guys carried and stuffed the truck. We kept finding things that had not been packed, and we began running out of boxes. The movers would not pack or carry any of the cleaning things in the kitchen, pantry, or bathrooms so we wound up stuffing those things into whatever bag or box we could find and putting them in our cars. When the big truck was loaded, we headed off to Kinde to repeat the previous day's craziness. The guys were in such a rush to finish, we could barely keep up.

One of the last things they had to do was put my bed together, but some of the pieces to the platform bed were missing. I slept on it with fear and trepidation for several nights, hoping it wouldn't fall down before Terry could rebuild it properly. We finally found the missing boards weeks later, taped together, marked "Sharon's bed," buried in the book boxes in the loft room. That was only one of so many weird things we discovered in the great unpacking.

When the crew left, Shannon managed to manipulate the boxes enough to move my chair in front of the television, so I could have some entertainment on my first night in my new home. It was kind of like camping out. The three rows of boxes stacked three high behind my chair were like the forts my kids built when they were young. I felt strangely protected and very happy to be home.

## THE UNPACKING

On Day 3 of the move, the unpackers arrived, three instead of the four we were promised and announced they could only work four hours instead of the whole day we had agreed on. Frustrated, we quickly regrouped and decided the kitchen, the pantry, and the wardrobe boxes would be first priorities. Shannon and two of the guys set up a very effective relay system. They unpacked the dishes, etc., and she put them into the cabinets. We had decided ahead of time where things should go. She did an amazing job of getting the whole kitchen and pantry unpacked in that short time. Meanwhile, my helper and I emptied the wardrobe boxes, hung the clothes and stuffed the extra things into the closets to be organized later. A month later, I was still working on that mess.

Our unpacking helpers left at noon on Sunday, taking the empty boxes with them. We were pleased we could actually see the carpet in places. We called it a win but couldn't call it a day. Don's niece, Teresa, and her husband, Larry, would be arriving that evening to spend the night before packing up the antique furniture the next morning and heading back to Kansas City. We managed to clear a path in the guest room, put sheets on the bed, and towels in the bathroom. I knew they wouldn't mind the boxes. We moved the living room boxes into the cleared dining room and created a space where we could sit and visit. When they arrived, we ordered Mexican dinners and had a fun evening together. They were as tired as me, so bedtime was early.

There would be no unpacking on Monday. The parade of people picking up furniture started at 9 a.m. Chris, Christopher, and Terry helped Teresa and Larry load Don's huge antique desk, the campaign chest, two chairs, a rocker, the clocks and miscellaneous things that had belonged to Martha, Don's mom. By 10, they were on the road, headed back to Kansas City.

Chris had accepted my offer of a dresser, a desk, the teak kitchen table, and two chests of drawers. With Terry's and Christopher's help, they were quickly loaded onto his trailer. Terry had agreed to take the wrought-iron deck furniture. That got carried out and loaded next.

As they were getting ready to leave, my neighbor from down the street and the president of the local Women's Club arrived to announce that she couldn't find anyone to pick up the things I had donated to the club for auction – the china cabinet, buffet, an antique gaming table with four chairs, and a rocking chair. I panicked because everything had to be out that day for the house cleaners and carpet cleaners to come in on Tuesday and Wednesday and the photographer on Thursday. The house would go back on the market on Friday. The schedule left no room for postponements.

As they have done for me so often, Chris and Terry came to our rescue and agreed to move and deliver the furniture to the clubhouse, which was only a few miles away. I breathed easier. In the middle of all that confusion, the Children's Hospital thrift store truck arrived to pick up leftover pictures and other miscellaneous things I had not been able to gift to friends. I had done my best, even having a Giveaway Night for my beauty consultants and other friends to carry away dishes, knickknacks, etc. I also offered things to the ladies who had cleaned the house before we put it on the market. The Woman's Club inherited numerous bags and boxes of Christmas decorations, dishes, and more dustibles for their auction, which funded a scholarship for a local student.

You'd think, at that point, everything would be gone, but there were still some odds and ends in the storage building, two ancient, very heavy television sets and some small pieces of furniture. Junkluggers were the last to arrive. We scoured the house and buildings to be sure everything remaining, left with them. I was happy to learn they try to donate anything useable to keep things out of the landfill. It was a little disconcerting to have to pay people to take things away. But we did, and it went, and Shannon and I would have done a happy dance if we hadn't been so tired.

But we weren't quite through. We had to finish clearing out under the kitchen sink and bathroom cabinets and we had to empty out the refrigerator, so all those things could be cleaned the next day. Then we went from room to room, double-checking closets, making sure we hadn't missed anything. Every time we thought we were finished, we'd find something else. Both of our cars were piled full when we finally locked the doors and staggered home to collapse.

There would be very little unpacking the rest of the week . Shannon went back to work after her week off to help me. I ran back and forth between houses to coordinate the house cleaning, carpet cleaning, photos for the ads, etc. I also spent a day with Chris, moving all my potted plants, and transplanting the things I wanted to keep – my peonies, iris, and lilies. We even moved some of the rocks Don and I had carried all the way from West Virginia to create borders all around the Tanbark yard. Chris and his son, Christopher, did the same thing at the new house, laying rock borders and planting all the flowers. My small patio in back is now a lovely little garden with huge pots of happy hostas. Every time I walk outside, I silently thank those wonderful guys for allowing me to keep some of the lovely growing things from my old home.

The empty, sparkling-clean Tanbark house went back on the market that Friday, with an open house scheduled for Saturday and Sunday. The house looked beautiful. Chris had pruned and mowed and mulched, so the outside was as pristine as the inside. We all had high expectations. This could be the week-end we found a buyer. But we didn't. Turnout was low, and there were no offers. We had been excited about a couple who wanted a space for horses, but at the last minute, the husband balked on moving, and it all fell through.

August ended, and September began with few showings. This journey I had started in May felt like it was never going to end. Chelle continued saying, "It only takes one. We just have to find the right one."

Meanwhile, I was spending all day, every day, with all those boxes. My new home began to take shape. I finished unpacking the living room, dining room, my bedroom, and tidied up the kitchen and pantry. The downstairs looked beautiful. I had left the upstairs for last, hoping the stairlift would be installed by then to make my running up and down easier. Finally, I got the call that October 3 would be the installation day. Because my staircase was higher than normal and curved, the stairlift had to be custom-built. It took longer than I'd hoped.

I knew the loft room would be the hardest room to unpack. There were so many boxes of books, plus all the Native American keepsakes. My friend, Becky, spent a whole day with me, unpacking the books and putting them on the shelves.

It was a big job, and I was so grateful for the help. I was fortunate to have other helpers, too. My girlfriend, Chris (different Chris), had helped me pack all my Mary Kay products and was brave enough to come back and help unpack them, too. She came at least once a week through September and helped me empty boxes. We made it fun, always including a decadent lunch and lots of laughs. Also, my friend, Suzanne, and her dad, Larry, spent a whole day helping me unpack all the books in my office. Terry was in and out, repairing this and that, painting the garage, and hanging pictures. I am so appreciative of all those people.

One of the things that excited me about the new house was the double garage. I needed a place to put all the things kept in our big storage building – seasonal decorations, seven years of tax returns, Christmas trees, etc. I was hopeful I'd be able to move the shelf units to the new garage and still have room to park my car empty through the winter.

I decided to make the garage a bigger priority than the upstairs. I spent days out there, unpacking and organizing. Shannon would come over after work and move out the empty boxes and help with anything I couldn't lift. Sometimes it felt like an impossible task. There was so much stuff, not just from the storage building but also the two other small storage rooms in the house. All now had to be squeezed into the garage. Once again, I filled garbage cans, donation boxes, and recycle bins, continuing to purge. Finally, on a 95-degree day in mid-September, the boxes were gone, the shelves were full and I could drive my car into my freshly painted (thanks to Terry) and organized garage. It was a triumph! A week later, we had a tropical storm, so we made it just in time.

About halfway through September, Chele and I conferred and decided, sadly, that we needed to lower the price of the house from $550,000 to $525,000 in hopes of generating more interest. It did help. There were more showings and a good turnout at open house. A young couple with two small kids expressed interest and made an offer of $485,000. I didn't feel I could go that low but decided, after much thought and lamenting, to counter with $500,000. They accepted, signed a contract and we began the process of inspections, qualification, etc. I had mixed feelings about the price but felt it wiser to accept a contract from someone who badly wanted the house than continue hoping someone else would come along and pay the full price I wanted. Most of the money was better than no money, I reasoned, especially as fall was approaching, and I didn't want the house setting empty through the winter.

The house inspection revealed some moisture in the attic that I was not aware of, but nothing else of any consequence. My buyers only asked that the roof be repaired. I agreed. That locked in the contract. We were one step closer to closing.

### The Stairlift - Part 2

After what seemed like a forever amount of waiting time, the stairlift installation day arrived, along with four smiling men and several neatly stacked piles of steel railing. At the end of the day, I had my first ride in my new chariot, which I had already dubbed Magic Mike. I was impressed with the efficiency, skill, and kindness of the guys who put the steel puzzle parts together and created this magic machine that was going to make my life so much easier. I had wondered if I would ever be able to say that the

$15,800 cost was worth it, BUT, it is.

*I'm feeling so at home and happy in my lovely new townhome, just one block from Shannon and A.J. Looking back, I was pleasantly surprised at how liberating it felt to clear everything out.*

# The Final Things

## THE BUYERS

After signing our contract, my buyers immediately put their house on the market and received an offer the first week-end. Our contract was contingent on that sale. They had twenty days to sell and close, which didn't seem like much time. But Chelle reassured me the house was adorable, in a desirable neighborhood, at an affordable price, so we crossed our fingers. We were disappointed to learn that first offer was not accepted, but a week later, they received another offer, accepted it, and tentatively scheduled their closing for November 1, which meant we could close on the Tanbark house on November 3. Happy dance!

## THE LAST BOX

The guest room was the last room left to unpack and maybe the worst, because I had piled all the things I didn't know what to do with in there. Took days to sort through, put away and finally, open that very last box, exactly two months from my move-in day. What a great feeling! We dubbed the room the Family History Room. I decided to fill the walls with family photos, starting with my grandparents' wedding picture and including my mom and dad's, Steven's, Shannon's and my own wedding photo. I added in lots of childhood snapshots of all of us, even me, and some fun ones of Steven and Shannon in their Colonial Williamsburg costumes. Steven was in the Fife and Drum Corps. Shannon was an interpreter in the colonial houses. I included the most recent photo of the grandkids, Adaline, Emma, and

Zachary to complete the circle. I have a framed poem in the midst of the photographs that reads:

> *"Our family is a circle of strength and love.*
> *With every birth and every union, the circle grows.*
> *Every joy shared adds more love.*
> *Every crisis faced together makes the circle stronger."*

As I was going through boxes, I found my high school yearbook. I decided to leave it out on the dresser for the grandkids to see when they come to visit. I thought they should see that Gramma was once young, too, and was quite a Kool Kat, as we used to say.

Scrapbooking is one of my favorite things to do. I created a large collection of scrapbooks from our travels. Where to put them was a big question. I didn't want them hidden away in drawers. Fortunately, the guest room closet was huge. Terry added shelves and created the perfect storage venue for my treasured books. I walked around, admiring each unique room, feeling so proud I'd actually been able to turn the empty space into this beautiful home.

I was overwhelmed with gratitude for all the helpers along the way, including Chelle, my savy realtor, whose letter to the neighborhood resulted in the purchase of the house.

Most of all, I couldn't possibly have managed this move at 80 years young without my daughter, Shannon, who worked with me every Saturday and sometimes Sunday, too, from May until the end of October, purging, hauling out stuff, packing, unpacking. Once I was in the house and the unpacking began, she came every day after work and carried out boxes, packing paper, etc. She also kept my refrigerator full and reminded me to stop long enough to eat at least three times a day.

No repayment is enough, but I'm hoping to send her and my son-in-law, A. J., off to the beach for a few days to rest up. At the beginning of the packing, moving process, A. J. developed severe abdominal pain and had to undergo hernia surgery, putting him out of commission for the duration. I teased him that it was a deliberate plan.

# THE ROCK

There once was a unique rock with a face carved into it that resided by my carport. After we moved all the garden pots and border rocks and created my beautiful little garden spaces, I realized Face Rock had not made the move. Chris and I both searched the Tanbark yard. No rock.

He then searched his garage and storage buildings, thinking maybe it had gotten mixed in with other things we had moved. We were both perplexed. How do you lose a big rock?? Sadly, as of this writing, Face Rock is still missing. Sigh…

# THE CLOSE, FINALLY

On a rainy Monday, six months from my momentous decision to sell and move, I signed the final papers, transferring the deed to 124 Tanbark Lane to the new owners, who are going to transform it into a forever home for them and their two children, ages three and five.

I remember the day I saw the house for the first time and called Don to tell him I'd found the perfect house for us. We signed the contract the same day and stayed awake most of the night, holding hands, planning, dreaming of the life we were going to build together in that house. We did, indeed, build a wonderful life there.

We filled the house with our travel treasures, planted flowers, shrubs, and flowering trees under the tall oaks and pines. Our friends came to visit from across the country and declared we had the best bed and breakfast in town. Our his and hers kids and grandkids filled the house on holidays and for no reason at all, except they loved to come there. We hosted Halloween parties, birthday celebrations, picnics and our own Red Letter Day surprise wedding. (That's a whole other story in my memoir, Daughter of the Mountains.)

I walked through the house on that last day and thanked it for all the joy it had given Don and me. The house has always been filled with love and laughter, and now it will be again as a new family creates their own story. I locked the door and drove away with no regrets.

As for me, I am comfy and happy in my beautiful new townhome, one short block from Shannon and A.J. Looking back, the biggest surprise was how liberating the clearing out was. That realization, early in the purging process, that I didn't need to keep the things to keep the memories, changed everything. After that, each item that went to a new home made me feel freer, happier.

I am proof that a new life can begin at any age, even eighty, and like the heroines in my favorite fairy tales, I plan to live happily ever after.

## Some Simple Down-Sizing Tips...

- Stop procrastinating and start!

- Tackle one area at a time – a drawer, a closet, a room.

- Be prepared with packing materials. Designate boxes, bags for Donations, Trash, Keep, and ???.

- Take photos of things you can't keep but want to remember. Make a scrapbook.

- Schedule a give away night for friends to come and carry away loot.

- Measure, measure to determine what furniture can go with you and what needs to be adopted.

- Consider consignment shops, libraries, thrift stores, charitable organizations for left-overs.

- Ask for help from friends, family, co-workers. Make worktime – fun-time.

- Absolve yourself of guilt for getting rid of things.

- Keep the items you love, pass the rest on to someone else to love and enjoy.

- Remember, it's all just stuff.

*Happy Downsizing!*

# About the Author

**Sharon Canfield Dorsey** is an award-winning poet and author. She has written four children's books, two memoirs, two books of poetry, an anthology, an Affirmation Journal, and a travel memoir.

"Writing is like breathing for me – necessary for survival. It's the first thing I want to do in the morning and the last thing I want to do at night."

She has been honored to have her work published in many anthologies and prestigious magazines like *The Pen Woman*, the publication of the National League of American Pen Women, alongside the work of such icons as Maya Angelou. She is a frequent contributor to *The Journal* (Writers Guild of Virginia).

https://www.sharoncanfielddorsey.com

# Books by Sharon Canfield Dorsey

*POETRY:*

* Walk with Me: The Poetry of Sharon Canfield Dorsey
* Tapestry: The Poems of Sharon Canfield Dorsey
* Captured Moments: The Poetry Anthology of the James City Poets

*CHILDREN'S BOOKS:*

* Revolt of the Teacups
* Buddy the Bookworm: Rescues the Doomed Books
* Herman the Hermit Crab: and the mystery of the big, black, shiny thing.
* Buddy and Ballerina Save the Library

*MEMOIR*

* Daughter of the Mountains
* Twenty-Four Months That Changed the World: and Us

*TRAVEL*

* Road Trip: A Love Letter to America
* Road Trippin': In the era of COVID-19

*AFFIRMATION JOURNAL*

* Begin Somewhere: The remarkable journal that allows you the freedom to start your journey when you decide it's a New Year.

I really hope this book has been helpful to you in some way. I would absolutely love to hear your thoughts about it. Honest reviews can make a big difference for other readers trying to find the perfect book for them. If you could take a moment to leave a review on Amazon. com, that would be fantastic! Here's how to do it:

Go to Amazon.com

In the search bar at the top of the page, type in the number 978-1-962935-03-6. It will look like this:

Press the enter key. My book will appear. Click on Ratings at the top of the page:

5.0 ★★★★★ ˅    2 ratings

**Customer reviews**
★★★★★ 5 out of 5

2 global ratings

| | | |
|---|---|---|
| 5 star | | 100% |
| 4 star | | 0% |
| 3 star | | 0% |
| 2 star | | 0% |
| 1 star | | 0% |

˅ How customer reviews and ratings work

**Review this product**

Share your thoughts with other customers

Write a customer review

The review screen will appear. At the bottom is a button "Write a customer review".

Click on this button and you will be prompted to write your review.

Thank you so much!

*Sharon*

Made in the USA
Middletown, DE
04 August 2024

58313207R00038